NATIONAL GEOGRAPHIC

# Time to Eat

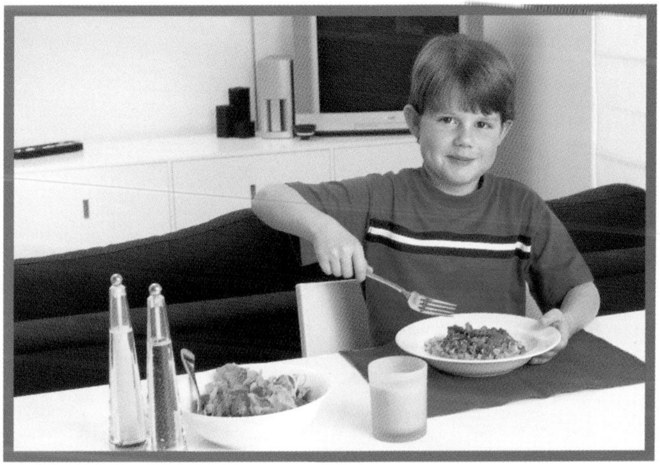

Jan Pritchett

# breakfast

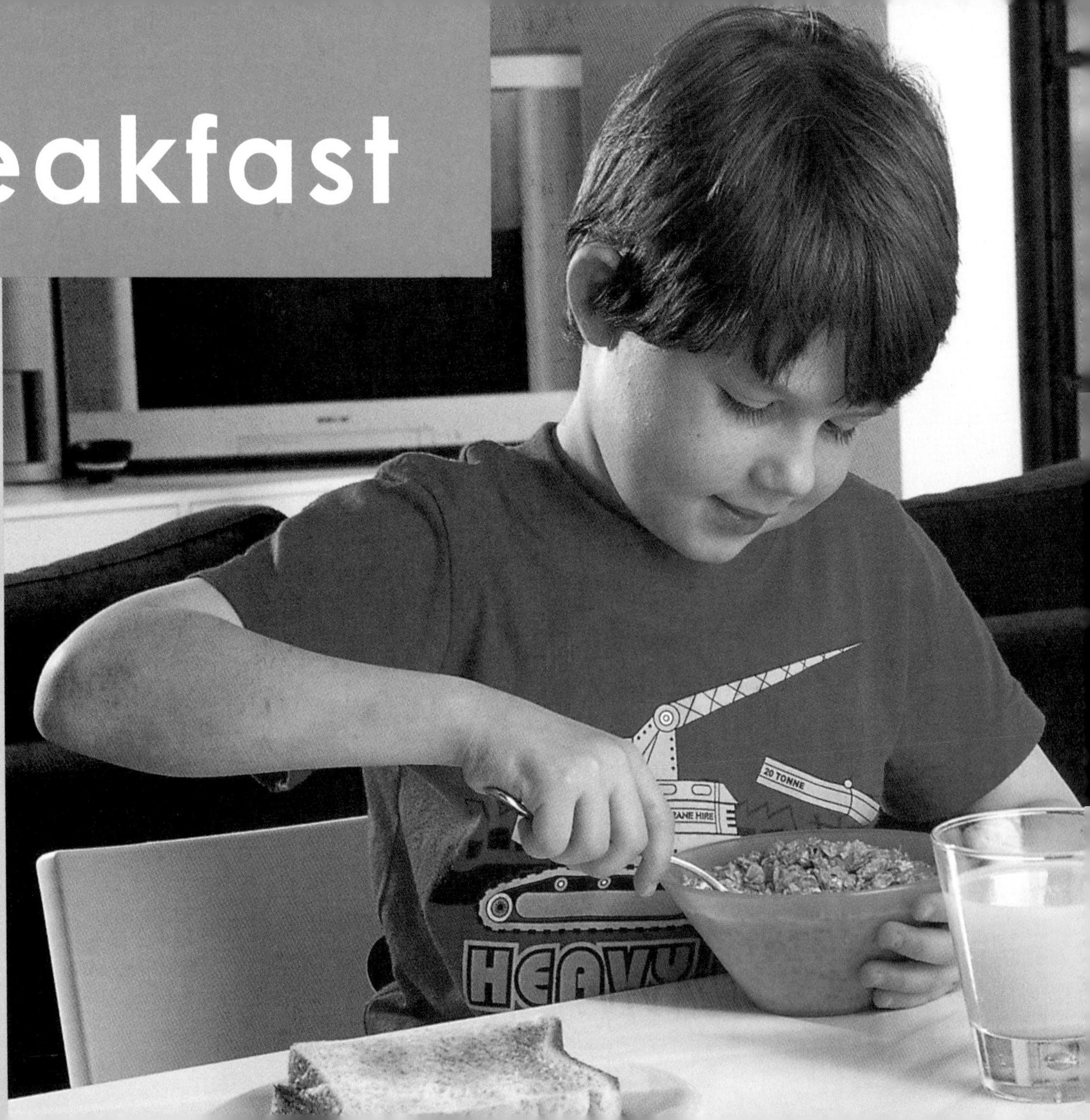

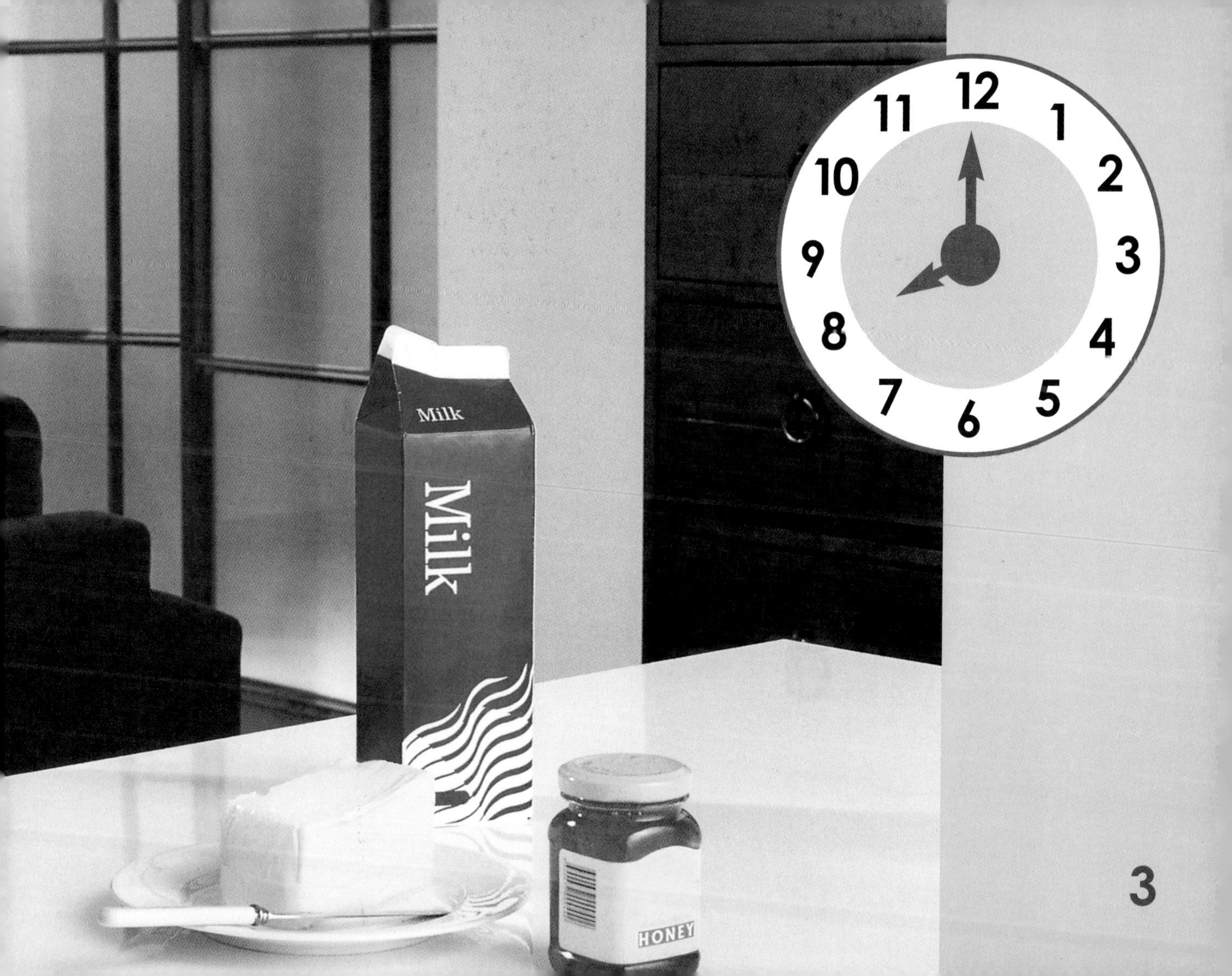
Milk
Milk
HONEY

# lunch

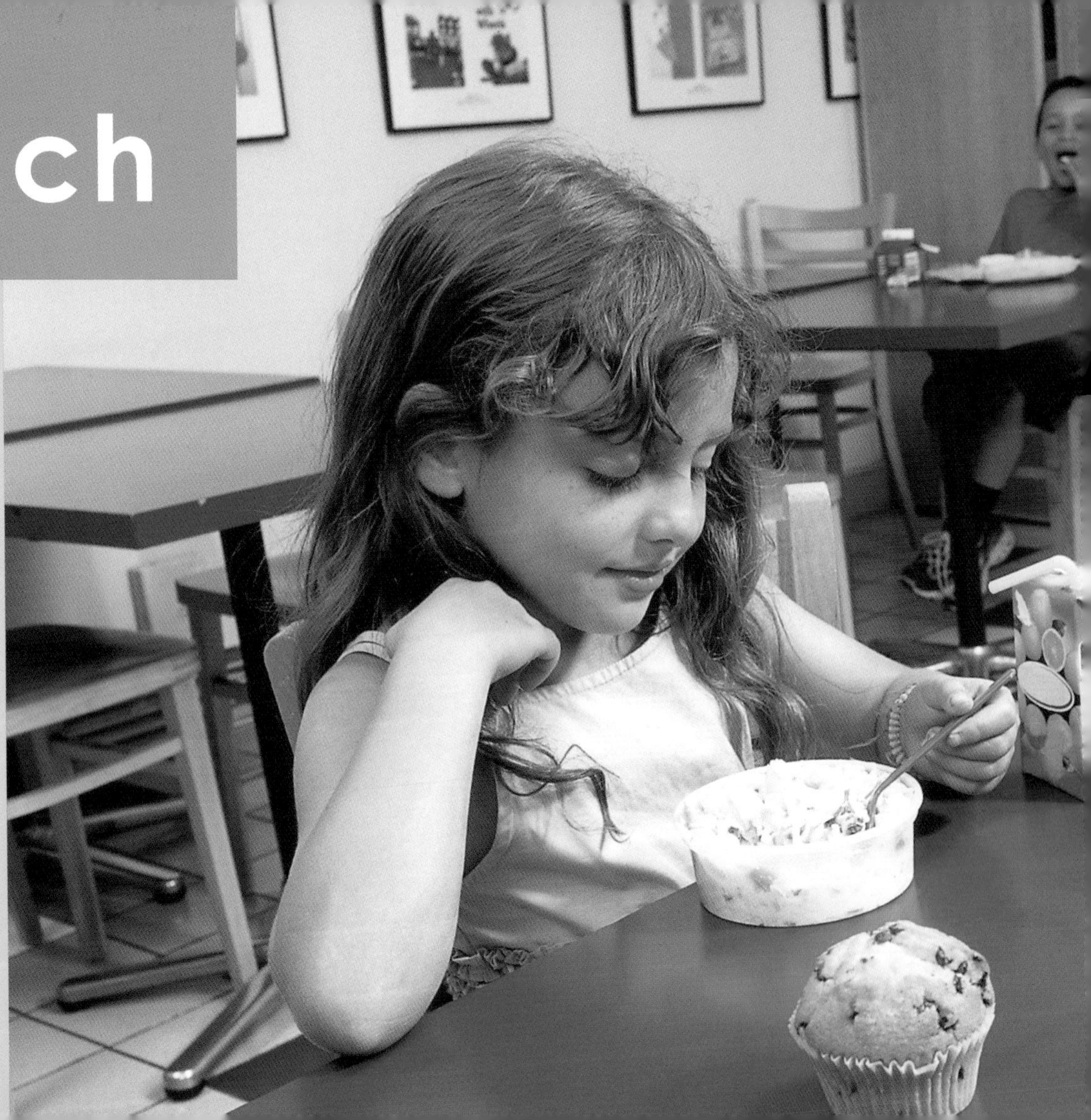

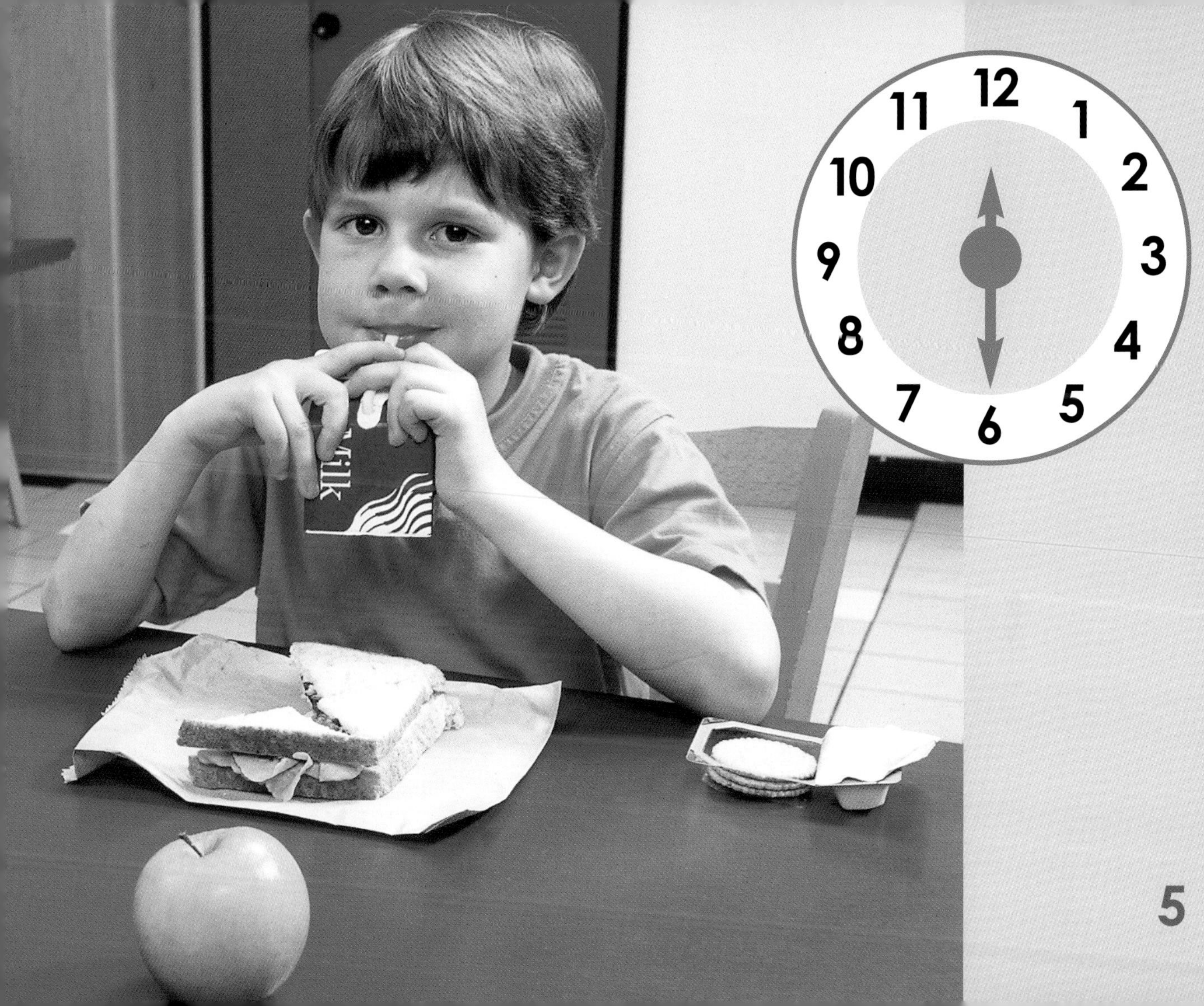
12
1
2
3
4
5
6
7
8
9
10
11

# dinner

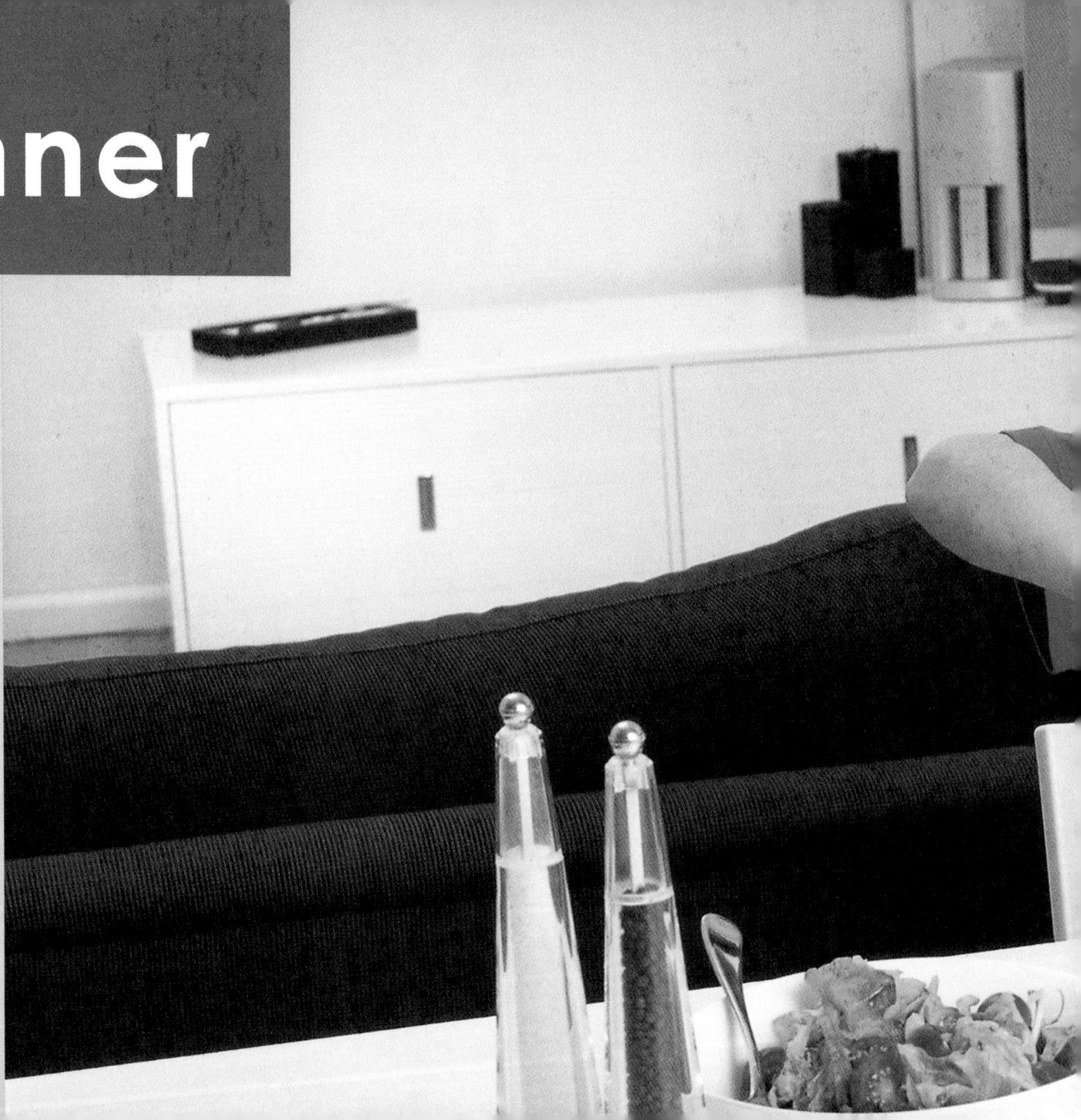

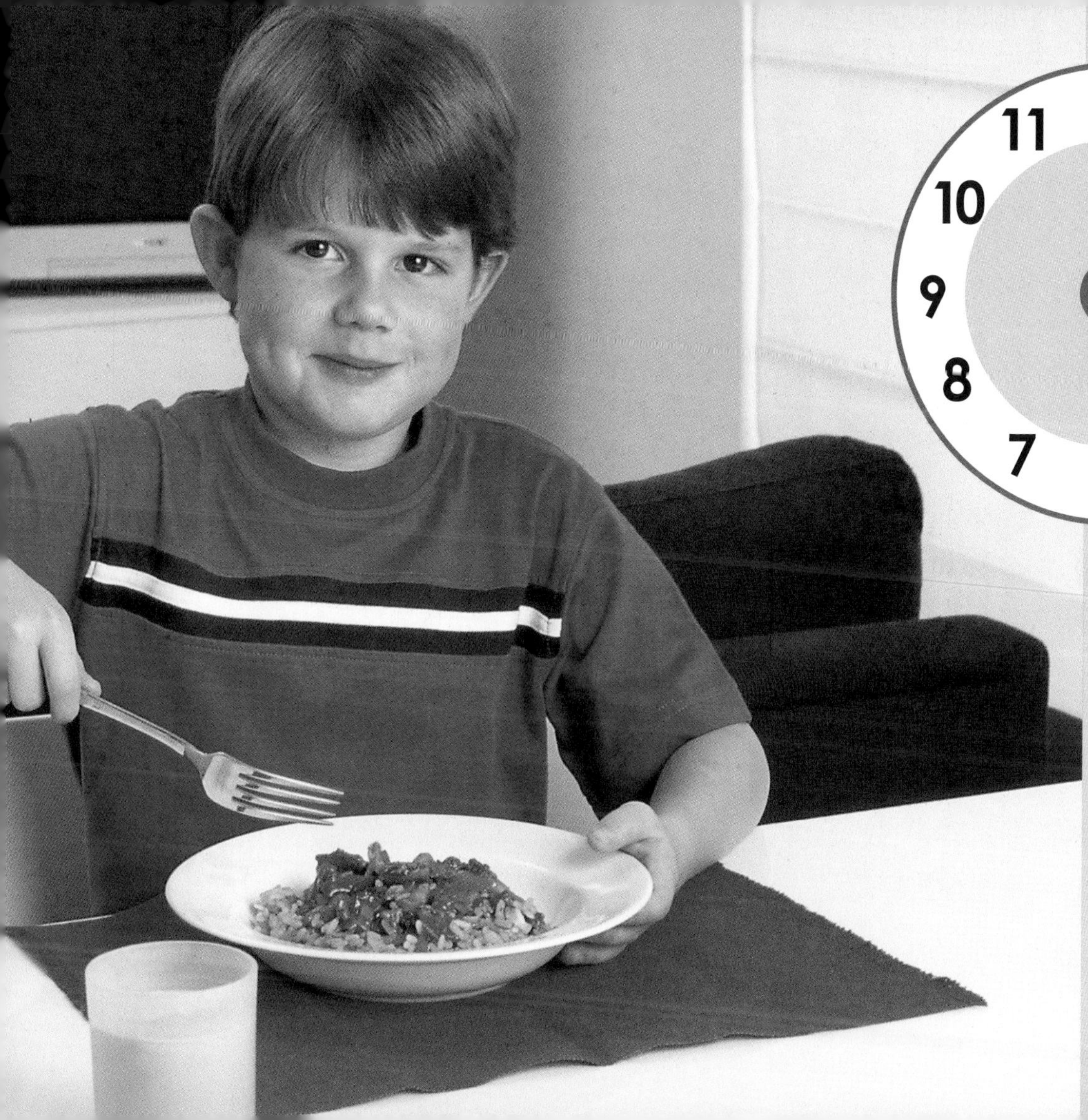

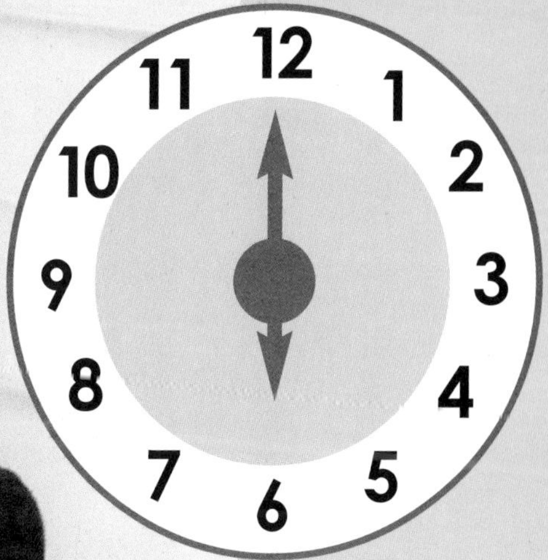
12
1
2
3
4
5
6
7
8
9
10
11

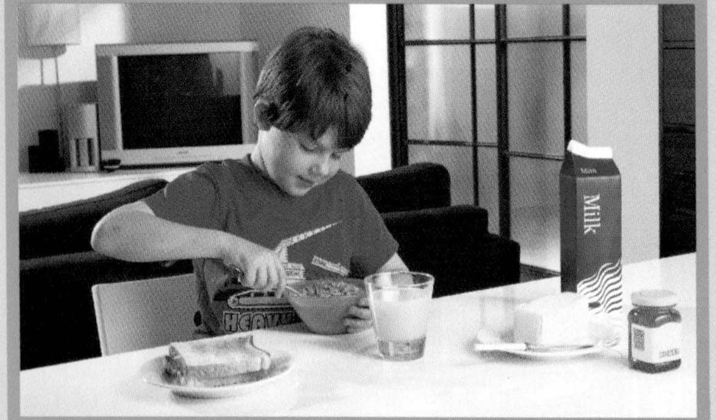


breakfast

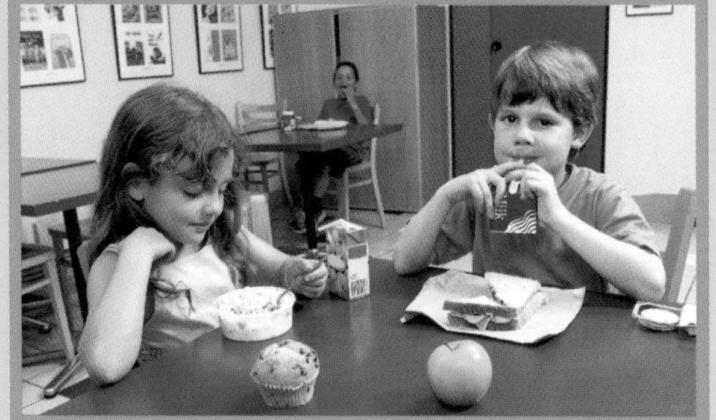

lunch

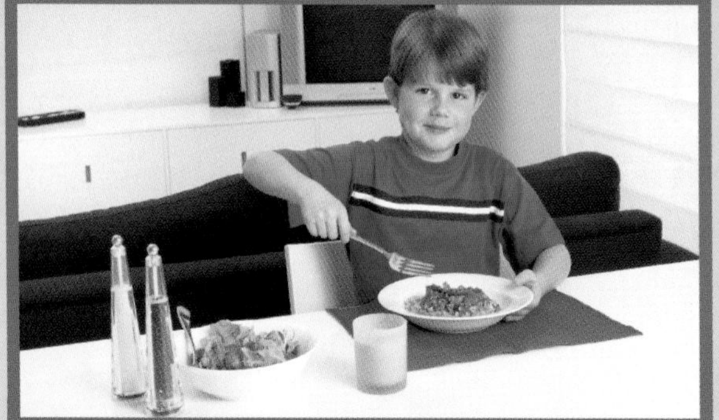

dinner